MW00927877

MINDFULNESS FOR BEGINNERS

Twenty-five Easy Mindfulness Exercises to Help You
Live in the Present Moment, Conquer Anxiety &
Stress, and Live a Fulfilling Life with Mindfulness
Meditation

Ella Marie

Table of Contents

INTRODUCTION

Mindfulness is a great place to be in your life. Instead of spending all that time working and hoping that you are going to get it all done, you will get to actually enjoy the things that are in your life. Mindfulness requires that you slow down and just realize what is going on near you and see that the little things in life are what make it all worthwhile. This is something that many people are going to forget about in their lives, and they often will feel anxiety, depression, and other issues because they are not connected to the life they are living. This guidebook is going to spend some time talking about mindfulness so you can see how big of an impact it can have on your life and make the decision on whether it is the right choice for you to try out.

Chapter 1 starts out with some information on what mindfulness is. You will understand the benefits of using these techniques, some tips on how to be more mindful, and so much more.

Chapter 2 starts out with mindful eating and how the simple act of eating could be a great experience.

Chapter 3 is about mindful listening. There are so many sounds that are going on around you all of the time, but it is easy to get busy with other things and not spend the time that is needed to really enjoy those sounds.

Chapter 4 is about mindful walking. This is when you pay attention to the way you walk as well as all of the things in nature that are around you. You will understand that the steps you take have a certain sound and that how far or fast you go can all make a difference.

Chapter 5 is full of the different exercises that you can do in order to try out mindfulness in your daily life. All of the exercises are easy to follow and you will be able to do them whenever you have a bit of time. Some just ask you to concentrate on the breathing that you are doing, while others are going to take a bit more effort. It is important to try and keep your mind on the task at hand rather than letting your mind wander. This is difficult to do at first, but with some practicing and repetition, it is going to become much easier.

There are many different types of mindfulness, including mindful eating, mindful listening, and mindful walking. There is also a variety of exercises that you will be able to do in order to reach the mindful state that you are looking for. Many of these are discussed in this book so that you can give them a try and see if they are going to work out for you. Take this book with you to learn some more about mindfulness and how it can be beneficial to your needs.

CHAPTER 1
WHAT IS MINDFULNESS?

Keeping control of the thoughts and feelings that you are going through can be really difficult. Most people find that they are going to struggle with this over time because there is too much that is going on in their lives that they are not able to keep up with. Mindfulness is a technique that you will be able to use in order to get your mind back on track so you can get the peacefulness that you have always wanted.

Mindfulness is known as the intentional and accepting focus of someone's attention on the sensations, thoughts, and emotions that are happening in that exact moment. It is going to take some practice in order to get this to occur in most people; it can become too easy to think about other things and let your mind wonder off rather than keeping it in one place. Often, the practice of mindfulness is going to be similar to what you will find in meditation in that you need to get your mind off the thoughts and feelings that are bothering it and get it to concentrate on what is going on right at that present moment.

There are a lot of uses to mindfulness. Psychologists have been using this practice for some time now in order to help patients deal with physical and mental conditions such as anxiety, obsessive compulsive disorder, and even drug addiction and depression. Even if you are not visiting a psychologist, it can be a nice exercise to use at home in order to properly handle your emotions in a more constructive manner.

BENEFITS OF MINDFULNESS TECHNIQUES

Many people decide to use mindfulness because it helps them feel better and get through their emotions more easily than if they just let the emotions run away. There are a lot of benefits that you can gain from using mindfulness exercises such as the following.

MINDFULNESS AND WELLBEING

These kinds of activities are going to be able to help you to improve your wellbeing. These exercises are able to support more positive attitudes that can lead to a happier and more satisfied life. When you start to employ mindfulness in your life, you are making it much easier to enjoy the pleasures that come into your life rather than being upset or worrying about other things when they occur. You will then be able to better deal with the bad events that occur because they will not seem like as big of a deal to you. When you train your mind to think in the present, you will often not worry as much about things that happened in the past because these things are just not that important to you anymore.

MINDFULNESS AND PHYSICAL HEALTH

You can also gain benefits to your physical health when you decide to employ mindfulness techniques in your life. The physical benefits include help with stomach troubles, better sleep at night, less chronic pain all over, a lowering of your blood pressure, better heart health, and much less stress. Just by reducing the amount of stress that you feel each day, you will soon be able to feel better about the other things that are going on in your life.

MINDFULNESS AND MENTAL HEALTH

Mindfulness techniques can help out the state of your mental health as well. There are many times when the stress and anxiety that you are feeling will start to creep into the other parts of your life and make things more difficult. This is where mindfulness can come in. It helps you to take control of your stress and other emotions so that you can have more rounded mental health without a lot of medication or other obstacles in the way. Some mental health conditions that can be helped with mindfulness include obsessive compulsive disorder, anxiety, couples' conflicts, eating disorders, substance abuse, and depression.

As you can see, there are a lot of benefits that you will be able to achieve for your whole body and health when you choose to practice mindfulness in your daily life. It is worth taking the time to learn a few exercises so that you are able to get it down and get back on track.

TIPS TO BEING MINDFUL

Here are a few tips that you can follow in order to have a better chance at being mindful either at a specific time or in your life in general.

MINDFUL BREATHING

This is a good one to start out with when you are not used to doing the mindfulness techniques but want to start using them each day. This is a simple exercise, but it can be really powerful when it is done correctly. You will start out with the in-breath and the out-breath, paying special attention to each one as they happen and recognizing that each one is different and special in its own way. The objective of this kind of mindfulness is that you will focus all of your attention on your breathing. The mental discourse might be there in the beginning, but over time it is going to fade away, and you will be able to notice this each time that you are being mindful.

This is not something that should be difficult or a lot of work for you to do. In fact, it is supposed to be enjoyable. You can think about how someone who is alive gets to enjoy breathing. Do not try to force the breathing; instead, let it come and go the way that it wants. If your out-breaths end up being longer than your in-breaths, this is fine. Just find the pace that is slow and steady but still works well for you.

This activity is a great one whether you are trying to be mindful, want to do a meditation session, or just need to calm down. There are so many benefits from simply taking in these deep breaths. Concentrating on them instead of on something else that might be bothering you can make life so much easier and more enjoyable.

CONCENTRATION

Once you have had time to get used to mindful breathing, you can take some time to get used to concentrating on it a bit more. You will just need to follow your breaths from their beginnings to their end. If your last in-breath went for four seconds, you need to make sure that the mindfulness lasts for its entire duration.

Concentrate just on the breathing that you are doing. You can just leave your breathing alone so that it ends up being as natural as possible, but you still need to focus your attention on it. This is probably going to be the most difficult part because it is easy to get distracted. The sound of the TV, the buzz of the dishwasher, remembering that you have an appointment next week for something—all of these thoughts can easily creep into your mind, and they will make it hard to concentrate.

Do not get discouraged; it is easy to have your mind wander when you are first getting started. Just stick with it and try to get rid of those other thoughts. It is going to get easier over time. Everyone has some trouble with this, so if you are able to just keep up with it, it will become much easier.

Spend some time getting used to concentrating on your breathing. You do not have to be an expert, but make sure you are comfortable with it, even if your mind still wanders a bit. At that point, you can move on to the next step.

BEING AWARE OF YOUR BODY

This activity is going to take it all a little bit further. You are going to not just pay attention to the way that you are breathing but also pay attention to your whole body. Realize that your body is there and breathing would not be possible without your body being there. As you breathe in, you should be aware of your body; as you breathe out, you should also be aware of your body. This is going to unite the body and the mind into one reality that is not able to be pulled apart.

When you are able to get your mind together with your body, you will find that you are well-established in the present instead of paying attention to the past or future. This is a good exercise to do if you are really stressed out about something and you are not able to get rid of the bad feelings.

This is a simple exercise, but it is going to be effective because it is going to bring your mind back to the here and now rather than letting it wander. Concentrating on things over which you have no control is just going to make you feel crazy. This exercise will make it much easier to concentrate on the present.

RELEASING TENSION

It is hard to let go of all the stress and tension that is going on in your life. You might have a lot of things to worry about at home or school or work, and these things are going to make you feel like you will always be stressed. It is normal for people to feel some stress, and often it is going to take some outside help in order to reduce tension.

Using mindfulness the right way is going to help you release the tension that you are feeling. You can choose to do these exercises in the way that is the most comfortable for you, whether it is in a standing, lying, or sitting position. No matter where you are, you might be able to get rid of the tension that you are feeling as long as you are able to figure out the best way to release it.

While you are breathing and doing the exercises that are listed above, you can say you are aware of your body as you breathe in and that you are ready to release tension when you breathe out. This breathing is going to make you feel better. Combine that with forgetting stressful thoughts and your tension will be released.

HOW TO BE MORE MINDFUL

Before you get started on your journey to being mindful, it is important that you take the time to figure out some tips to help you get started. These tips are going to make it easier to do mindfulness in the proper way so that you are getting all of the benefits that you would like out of this technique. Some of the tips that you should follow include:

- **Put the right value on things**: It is easy to become stressed out over how much something costs or how much better it will make you look. When you put a value on things, it is only going to end up stressing you out even more. When you let go of this kind of value on things, you open up your world to pleasure and having more fun in life.
- **Stay neutral or expect the best**: It is easy to be negative about the things that are going on in your life. You may be afraid of the future because of your past. Stay positive about your situation the whole time. This can make life much happier and easier to deal with.
- **Be nice and use compliments**: This allows you to make a difference in someone else's life. When you are worried about making someone else feel better, you will tend not to think about your own life as much, and the little things that have been bothering you will not seem as important any longer. Try to give at least a few compliments each day to help make those around you feel better.
- **Observe yourself**: Take some time each day to observe the way you are doing things. Figure out if the way you breathe seems to be out of sync with the way you think you are feeling. When you take a few minutes to concentrate on your breathing, you start to become aware of the things that are going on in your body,

and you can start to make conscious efforts to control them better.

- **Spend time with friends and on relationships**: Nothing is going to make you feel better than when you spend time with your family and friends. These are the relationships that make you feel good and give you a sense of self-worth. You should spend as much time as you can developing these relationships while you are working on your mindfulness so that you can feel your very best at all times.

CHAPTER 2
MINDFUL EATING

One of the areas that you will be able to concentrate on your mindfulness is when you are eating. It is easy to just scarf down your food and not even think about it. You will be in a hurry to get the meal done because you have to get back to work or you just are hungry and want to finish. But when you practice mindful eating, it is much easier to enjoy the food that you are eating.

So, what is mindful eating? This is eating that requires you to eat with an intention of taking care of yourself rather than eating just because you think you should be eating. You can use this method to make the meal taste better, to enjoy it more, and to make sure that you are eating just when it is needed. This can help you to eat what the body needs instead of loading it up with foods that are just too much for it.

To start with, you should sit down with your plate of food at the table. Make sure that you do not have any outside distractions while you are doing this. Anything that can take your mind off this task will make it pretty much impossible to get the full mindfulness that you are looking for. Turn off the TV, get rid of the morning paper, and spend your time thinking about and enjoying the food that you have in front of you.

There are some things that you should keep in mind when you are doing this activity. You will not be allowed to gobble down the food that you will be eating. Instead, you must make sure to take slow and deliberate bites for each mouthful. You will then be better able to pay full attention to all of the food you are eating, taking in how it looks, how it smells, how you cut it up, the muscles that were used to get it to your mouth, the taste and texture of the food, and everything else. You should try to become fully involved in the process of eating in order to truly enjoy it.

It might seem like this is going to be a slow and laborious process, but you will soon be amazed at how much you will be able to enjoy the food that you are eating when you start to do this. This method of eating will fill you up faster and is much better for your digestion.

Here are some of the steps when it comes to mindful eating:

- Pick out a small food piece and start with that.
- Explore it using as many of your senses as you can. Look at the food for a bit and notice the color and the texture that comes with the food.
- Once that is done, you can close your eyes before spending time using the sense of touch to explore the food. How does the food feel without looking at it? Would you be able to

describe it to another person who is not able to see?

- Now it is time to use the sense of smell. See what the different smells are that come with the food.
- Eat the food. You should take a minimum of two bites for each piece of food, even if it is a small piece. It is easy to take big bites and barely chew, but you will not be getting the mindfulness out of it, and this could be making you feel sick and still hungry.
- With the first bite, chew slowly and notice how much of a sensory experience you are getting out of this exercise just by taking the time to chew and taste your food. Feel the texture of the food and the way that it feels inside your mouth. Notice how intense the flavor is with each bite. You should take at least twenty to thirty seconds to eat the first bite to enjoy all of the flavoring.
- You do not have to eat this slowly each time you have a meal, but for the first few times trying out the mindfulness technique, it can really make a difference. It can help you to slow down with your regular eating so that the process becomes easier.

This is a great way to improve your life and actually enjoy the little things that are in it. It becomes way too easy for people to throw their food down their throats and not even think about it. Not only are you not able to enjoy the food that you are eating this way, you could also cause stomach and digestive issues. Try to do this quick exercise a few times a week and see how much it helps.

NEW FOODS

Try out some new foods. It is easy for people to take one quick bite of a new food and decide whether they like it or not. They are not really taking the time get to know the food, to really taste it, or to actually figure out if they like it or not. Use mindful eating each time you try new foods so that you can really experience them.

BENEFITS OF MINDFUL EATING

There are a lot of benefits that you will be able to get out of using mindful eating in your daily life. Some of the benefits include:

- **Prevention of diabetes**: There have been studies done that show how eating too fast, something that many Americans do in their typical diet, can cause diabetes. This is because you are more likely to gain weight when you eat this way.
- **Prevent obesity**: Binge eating can be a concern with adults as well as children. This can be caused by a strict diet and weight gain.

When you work at mindful eating, you will have more control over your eating habits.

- **Stop excessive snacking**: It is easy to multi-task while you are eating, but studies show that when you just concentrate on your food rather than doing something else, it can make you less hungry throughout the day and you might pick out smaller snacks.

- **Prevent overeating**: When you go out to eat, it can be easy to eat more food than you should, which can make it easier to gain weight. These foods will have more calories than your normal foods, which is going to keep adding more onto your daily total. When you use mindful eating, you will not have all of these extra calories adding on.

- **Stay lean**: When you are eating fewer calories, which is something that will happen when you practice mindful eating, you will be able to become leaner. This makes it the perfect thing to try when you want to lose weight.

CHAPTER 3
LISTENING

Not only are you able to become mindful about the things that are going on around you, but you will also be able to do this kind of thing when it comes to listening. Often, life can get really busy, and it can be difficult to really listen. It is easy to go to work, come home, go on a walk, and do so many other things without ever hearing the sounds that are around you.

When you take the time to listen mindfully, you are making sure that you are actually hearing these amazing sounds. When you race out of the house to get to work, do you notice the sound of birds chirping? If you are like most people, then you probably do not. When you take the time to listen, it becomes easier to appreciate everything life has to offer.

Here are a few of the exercises that you can do in order to practice a little bit of mindful listening in your day.

EXERCISE #1

Stop right now, no matter what you are doing, and take a notice of the sounds that might be surrounding you. It does not matter if you are in the office, on the ride to work or school, out with friends, or doing some other activity; just stop what you are doing and listen. There could be a million different sounds that are surrounding you, but humans have learned how to ignore most of them either due to necessity, because they are too busy with other things, or just because they would probably go insane if they noticed every sound around them all day long.

While you are doing this exercise, see how many different things you are able to identify as noises. Do you hear the computer humming next to you or a car passing by somewhere in the distance? You might hear the television that is on in another room. If the window is open, you could hear the birds a bit or the sound of rushing water or a nice breeze. What you hear will depend on where you are. You will most likely be surprised by all of the different sounds that you are able to hear when you take the time to listen.

Does this sound like an exercise that is pretty easy to do? You will be amazed at how difficult it is to actually concentrate on the noises rather than letting your mind wander. You need to try to envelop yourself in the noise that is around you instead of trying to block it out.

EXERCISE #2

This is going to be a timed listening method. With this one, you are going to come up with the amount of time that you will do this activity. It might be best to do this activity at home when you do not have any extra distractions so that you do not have to worry about being interrupted.

It is best to start out with just five minutes or so on this activity and you will always be able to add on as time goes on and you get used to it. Set a stop watch so that you only need to pay attention to the sounds around you rather than worrying about how much time has passed. Now let the sounds anchor you to the present moment. Do not judge, analyze, or even think about what could be causing each of the sounds as you hear them, just experience and observe them. If you find that you are becoming impatient or restless during your time, do not react to those feelings.

Doing this simple exercise is going to make your awareness open up on a whole new level when it is compared to the silence that is inside of you. You will experience some times when you start to feel like you are waking up to a new part of you that has been hidden and that you will now be able to enjoy.

EXERCISE #3

This is one that is going to help you with listening. Often people will find that it is really difficult to get their minds to stay on task. One way that you can do this is by using mindfulness bells. These have been used for many years in order to give the person a focal point of concentration for their mindfulness meditation.

With this exercise, you will be listening to a recording of the mindfulness bells instead of just listening to all of the sounds that are going on around you. This is nice because it is often easier to concentrate when there is just one sound. It can also make the process more powerful and deeper.

If you are new to the process of meditation or mindful listening, this is the best way to get used to doing it. It is going to be difficult to get your mind to concentrate on just one thing. Thoughts and feelings are often going to get in the way, making it tough to concentrate on the things that are right in front of you. But think about how much more control you will have over your emotions and feelings if you are able to control them with the use of mindful listening.

EXERCISE #4

If the bells are not quite your thing and you find that they are distracting you, it is always fine to use some other method or sounds that can help. Perhaps pick out your favorite song or a classical song. Classical songs are usually the best because they have a lot of different instruments and sounds that you can envelop yourself in, and they are easy on the ears so you will not get distracted.

Turn on the song of your choice and just listen to it. You should listen to the different melodies and take note when something changes. Listen to the different instruments and see if your favorites are among them.

There is so much that you can enjoy when it comes to music: lyrics, instruments, melodies, and more.

Mindful listening is an important thing that you should learn how to do and that you should combine with some of your exercises when you are trying to be more mindful. There is so much that is going on around you that only your ears are able to pick up on. With busy schedules and all of the noises bombarding us, it is easy to ignore the sounds and not pay attention to them. These exercises help you learn how to pay attention to at least some of these sounds so that you can become more aware of what is going on around you.

CHAPTER 4
MINDFUL WALKING

Walking is a great activity that you can do in order to get out of the house, have some fun, get some movement, and even lose some weight if you would like. Many people try to add in more walking to their lives because of all the positive health benefits. But, did you know that you can also bring mindfulness into your walking routine to make it better?

A lot of the same principles are going to come into play when you do your mindful walking. In this activity, you are simply going to focus your mind on the act of walking, even if it is such a simple thing to understand. During this process, you are going to learn how to bring your awareness into the movement of the body as you are walking. There is so much that goes into each step that is taken that it is easy to find a way to spend your energy concentrating on it all.

As you are walking, you should concentrate on how the ground feels or how you breathe. Are your steps brisk or slower? Is your breathing on par with your exercise or will you need to pick up a heavier speed for results? You can also take the time to concentrate on the things that are going on around you, such as birds flying, dogs playing, or something else.

With this exercise, you are not going to need to spend a lot of time ignoring the things that are going on around you; in fact, you will be able to concentrate on some of these as you are walking in order to get more out of the experience.

One of the best things about this kind of mindfulness is that you will be able to do it at a moment's notice, no matter where you are. With some of the other techniques, you are going to need to be alone and plan ahead a little bit. With this one, you can do it whenever. That is why there are so many people who like to use the walking technique when they are first trying out mindfulness.

CHAPTER 5
OTHER MINDFULNESS EXERCISES

In addition to some of the exercises that have been listed in the previous chapters, here are a few more that you can tryout in order to really bring mindfulness into your life. Try out a few to see how they will work for your needs.

ONE MINUTE MINDFULNESS

The first exercise that we will look at is the one minute mindfulness. This is one that you will be able to do at any time of the day, and since it does not take very long, you will not have to worry about setting aside a lot of time in your busy schedule. You can use your watch or set a quick timer to help you keep track of how much time you need to spend on this so that you can fully concentrate on the activity.

During the sixty seconds of this activity, you need to focus all your attention on your breathing. You should not think about anything else, pay any attention to anything else, or worry about other things that are going on. The only thing that should be in your universe during this minute is the breathing. While a minute might not sound like it is that long of a time, it can certainly feel like it lasts forever when you are getting started. You can leave your eyes open for this and breathe the way that you normally do; nothing has to change in order to do this exercise. You will have to be prepared to catch your mind when it tries to wander off, which it will, and keep bringing it back to where it needs to be. You will find that focusing your concentration like this in the beginning is going to be difficult, but the more you do it, the easier it will become.

While this is not one that is going to take a lot of time or that much effort, it is usually a really powerful one if you actually take the time to do it right. It can sometimes take people a long time of doing this exercise before they are able to do it for just the single minute. The good news for you is that if it is difficult, you can realize that a lot of other people are going through the same thing and that if you keep trying, it is going to become so much easier.

This is an exercise to do a few times through your day, especially if your mind is running off and you are not able to stay focused on the task that is at hand. You will be able to get the clarity and peace that you want, and soon things will be back on the right track. Over some time and with practice, you can choose to extend the amount of time for which you are doing this technique so that it works the best for you, but in the beginning, the minute is going to be hard enough for you to complete.

CONSCIOUS OBSERVATION

Even when you are observing things, you will be using some form of mindfulness to help you out. This exercise is going to help you out with using the practice of observation to help keep your mind sharp.

To get started, you should pick up some object that is just lying around; the object that you choose is really not that important, so pick up the first thing that you can find. You should hold the object in your hands and then allow your full attention to become absorbed into the object. Observe the object, but do not take the time to think about it or assess it, or study it in any way. Just look at it and observe it for what it is.

During this exercise, you will start to feel a higher sense of newness. Conscious observation has been known to make people feel more awake. You will begin to notice how the mind is able to quickly release all of its thoughts about the future or the past and how it feels so much different to be in this moment. This can also be considered a form of meditation, and many people will treat it this way.

This can also be done with the ears in the form of listening mindfulness like what was discussed in a previous chapter. You can choose the method that works out the best for your needs.

TOUCH POINTS

This is an exercise that is going to help you appreciate the little things that are in your life because it can help you slow the pace of what is going on around you. You will learn how to have a more pure awareness and will also be able to rest in the present moment for a bit.

When you are ready to do this exercise, you can sit down and think about something that has happened more than once for you every day. It should be something that you will take for granted, something like opening up a door or walking down the hall. We will go with opening the door. Think about the action of opening the door and allow yourself to feel how it is happening. Feel the door knob in your hand, how it feels to turn the knob, and how heavy the door is when you pull on it.

While you are thinking about all of this, think about the movements and the parts of your body that let you do these things. Be appreciative of the hands that are allowing you to do this, the feet that got you to the door, and the brain that told your body how to do the different things. Without these things, you would never be able to do a task as simple as opening the door.

The cues that you are using for this exercise do not have to include just physical ones. You could think about the negative thoughts that you might have throughout the day. Take a moment to think about the thoughts and then release them before they have more of an impact on your life. You can think about how food smells and take a moment to be thankful that you have some food that you can eat.

It does not matter what cue you choose to use. You should choose one that is going to resonate with you and make it easier to think in the proper way. You do not have to stay on autopilot all the time. Using this appreciation and method of thinking about simple actions can really make you feel better and help you get out of the rut of doing everything the same way each day.

COMES IN FIVES

This is a fun game that makes you think in terms of the things that are already in your life. You should take a few minutes to notice at least five things that are present in your day. These need to be things that you usually do not notice or that you do not take the time to appreciate. They can also be things that you see, feel, smell, or hear.

There are a lot of things that you can consider for this exercise. For example, you could see the walls that are in your home, hear all the birds on your drive to work, feel how your clothes feel on your skin, or smell some flowers that are in the park. These are things that you are not usually going to notice.

Take the time to allow your mind to explore the possibilities, impact, and wonder of these things. Allow your mind to open up and become awake to the world as well as the full experience that comes with noticing the environment.

When you are able to become more mindful of the person that you are, the things that are around you, and even the things that you are doing, you will start to see that everything in your environment has a purpose and is connected.

Try to do this exercise a few times each week, if not more, so that you can start to appreciate more things that are going on around you. It is possible to do this room-by-room in your home, at work, at church, in your car, or in any other place where you spend time. This is going to make it easier to start appreciating the things that are going on in your life so that you are able to feel more mindful and connected with your life.

TEN SECOND COUNT

This is a mix between the mindfulness that you are looking for and a way to practice concentration, and it is similar to the first exercise discussed. In this exercise, you are going to focus on closing your eyes and counting to ten. If you find that your concentration is wandering off, you will just start back at the beginning with the number one.

A lot of people find that this is an exercise that they are able to do a little bit better than the first one. This is due to the fact that they actually have something more concrete to concentrate on, rather than having to try and pay attention to breathing. The mind is not as likely to wander off.

BODY SENSATIONS

For this exercise, you should find a quiet place where you can sit in peace for at least five or ten minutes. You are going to want to sit still and notice the different sensations, such as an itch, which you should take the time to think about rather than scratching it immediately. Start from your head and notice the sensations there, and slowly make your way down to your feet and toes.

EMOTION NAMING

There are a lot of emotions that you could be experiencing in your life. It is easy to let them get in your way and influence the way that you think and act. But this is not the way to make sound decisions and to be in control of your whole life. For this exercise, you should allow all of your emotions that you are feeling at that moment come forward and look at them without judgment. You can then calmly name off the emotions that you are feeling, accept them, and then let them go.

Try to keep your mind on the exercise that is at hand. It can be difficult because you might want to let other thoughts and feelings get in the way. But you need to be able to concentrate on the sensations that you are dealing with in order to properly use the technique of mindfulness and to start realizing all of the little things that are in your life.

URGE SURFING

This is a good exercise to do if you are dealing with an addictive personality or you want to get over an addiction that you are dealing with. You will be able to better cope with the cravings that you are having and then let them pass by you. Notice how the body is feeling when the craving enters the body. Instead of wishing for the cravings to leave you, think about how they will soon subside.

MINDFULNESS CUES

For this particular exercise, you will need to be able to focus your attention on the breathing you do whenever certain cues show up in your environment. An example of this would be whenever a phone rings, you should bring some attention to your breathing in the present moment. You do not have to change your breathing, just be aware of the way that you are breathing and see if there is anything off or different about it.

You can choose a cue that is going to work for you, such as looking in a mirror, touching your hands together, or when you hear birds sing outside your window. It does not matter what the cue is as long as you take the time to recognize that cue and spend a little time being mindful about it.

The reason that you would use these cues in order to do a mindfulness exercise like this one is that they are a great way to get you out of the autopilot that life can often put you in. It is easy to keep going through life without much change and without realizing that things are going on around you. When you do exercises like this one, it becomes easier to keep up with life, realize how great it is, and be more in the moment.

OTHER MINDFULNESS OPTIONS

There are a lot of other things that you can do in order to be mindful in your daily life. The more you are able to practice this kind of technique, even if you are only able to do it for a few minutes each time, the more you are going to become present, worriless, and connected to the world. Some of the ideas that you can try in order to be more mindful include:

- Mind how your feet move while you are at the store getting groceries. This is going to allow you to see the different ways that you move while you are doing various activities. You are sure to walk in a different manner when you are shopping compared to when you are going around the office, doing a workout, or hurrying to get somewhere.
- Mind the feel of your chair while you are working on typing up a document. Chances are, you have never really thought that much about the chair that you are sitting in.
- Going through a door can be a mindful exercise. You can think about the feeling and the work that goes into pulling open the door. You can focus on

the task that needs to be done while you are going through the door. There are many ways you can be mindful of this.

- Switch around your shoes. You will usually have one shoe that you are going to put on first each day. Take the time one day to put on the opposite shoe first. You will be surprised at how much difference this simple gesture makes.

- Don't put sugar in your tea. This might sound kind of silly, but if you are used to putting sugar in your tea, it is going to make a difference in your routine. You can go the other way as well; if you do not usually add sugar to the tea, add some in this time. You can do this with your daily cup of coffee as well. This exercise is going to help you learn about patterns and understand how difficult it is going to be to break them. You do not necessarily want to change the pattern that you are used to; you just want to develop some more flexibility in your life.

- Breathe consciously when you have time. This can be anytime—when you are waiting for a meeting, waiting in line at a store, or waiting for your computer to start up. It does not matter when, just try to spend a little bit of time each day breathing in a way that makes you think about it.

- Clean up the house. Cleaning up your house is the perfect time to concentrate on being mindful. Think about all the areas of your home while you are cleaning them and determine what makes them so special and important in your life. Think about the items that you are picking up, and find out if they mean something to you.

- Keep a diary. This is a good way for you to take the time to think about your thoughts and find out if they are valuable. The goal is not to make the next piece of literature. It is more to observe the things that are going on around you and how they make you feel. It does not matter if it starts to feel repetitive in the process. This is something that you can expect, and the journal is just going to reflect the way that you see and feel about things.

- Notice things. Take in deep breaths and notice the things that are around you. This has been mentioned for the other exercises, but the idea cannot be stressed enough. You are not going to be able to think in a mindful way if you are not able to realize and appreciate the good things that are going on in your life, especially the things that you have not noticed in the past. Notice a few things that you are able to feel, then notice a few things that you are able to hear, and finally notice a few things that you are able to see.

- Just smile. This might seem like something that is simple, but it can make a big difference in the way you feel about what is going on in your life. Anytime you are annoyed, frustrated, or impatient, you should just smile. This is going to put you more at ease and make it easier to realize it is not the end of the world.

These are just a few of the mindfulness exercises you can use to get your mind off the past and future and back to the present so that you can enjoy what you have in life. While it is going to take some time to get used to, it is going to make your life so much better if you stick with it and make it work out for you.

CONCLUSION

There are a lot of benefits that come with living a life that is mindful. You will be able to enjoy the little things so much more and also help many of the health conditions that you might be going through that you did not even realize were connected. This book is meant to give you some more information about the mindfulness technique, what it is all about, why you should consider it, the different types of mindfulness, and some exercises that you can try out in order to get mindfulness to work out for you.

After having read this book, you should have a more thorough understanding of the physical and mental uses of mindfulness. Some of the techniques discussed were mindfulness while breathing, walking, and eating, all of which tune you in to your sensations and surroundings. Proper utilization of these techniques can lead to a happier, healthier, more fulfilling life. You can use the information contained within this book to stop taking things for granted and to learn how to appreciate even the smallest details of everyday existence.

DID YOU LIKE "MINDFULNESS FOR BEGINNERS"?

Before you go, I'd like to say thank you so much for purchasing my book.

I know you could have picked from dozens of books on this subject, but you took a chance with mine, and I'm truly grateful for that.

So, once again, a big thanks for downloading this book and reading all the way to the end—I truly appreciate it.

Now I'd like to ask for a small favor if you don't mind:

Would you be so kind as to take a minute of your time and leave a review for this book on Amazon?

This feedback will help me continue to write the kind of books that help you get results. And if you loved it, then please feel free to let me know! :)

Made in the USA
Lexington, KY
07 January 2017